Wilma Rudolph
Track and Field Champion

Adrianna Morganelli

 Crabtree Publishing Company
www.crabtreebooks.com

Author: Adrianna Morganelli

Series research and development: Reagan Miller

Editorial director: Kathy Middleton

Editor: Crystal Sikkens

Proofreader: Janine Deschenes

Photo researchers: Samara Parent and Crystal Sikkens

Designer and prepress technician: Samara Parent

Print coordinator: Katherine Berti

Photographs:
AP Photo: ©AP Photo: cover, pages 12-13, 24; ©William J. Smith: page 20; ©John Russell: page 29

Getty Images: ©ullstein bild: title page; ©Bettmann: pages 4-5, 21, 22, 23; ©George Silk: page 6, 18, 19; ©Mondadori Portfolio: pages 10-11; ©Jerry Cooke: page 15, 30; ©The Asahi Shimbun: page 25; ©Jodi Cobb: page 27

The Image Works: ©Sean Sprague: pages 8-9; ©histopics/ullstein bild: page 16; ©Schirner/ullstein bild: page 26

NBC/Photofest: page 28

Photoshot: ©TALKING SPORT: page 17

Public Domain: page 14

Wikimedia Commons: ©EVula: page 7

All other images from Shutterstock

Library and Archives Canada Cataloguing in Publication

Morganelli, Adrianna, 1979-, author
    Wilma Rudolph : track and field champion /
Adrianna Morganelli.

(Remarkable lives revealed)
Includes index.
Issued in print and electronic formats.
ISBN 978-0-7787-2689-0 (hardback).--
ISBN 978-0-7787-2700-2 (paperback).--ISBN 978-1-4271-1810-3 (html)

    1. Rudolph, Wilma, 1940-1994--Juvenile literature. 2. Runners
(Sports)--United States--Biography--Juvenile literature. 3. Women
runners--United States--Biography--Juvenile literature. I. Title.

GV1061.15.R83M67 2016   j796.42092   C2016-904104-2
                                                   C2016-904105-0

Library of Congress Cataloging-in-Publication Data

Names: Morganelli, Adrianna, 1979-
Title: Wilma Rudolph : track and field champion / Adrianna Morganelli.
Description: New York : Crabtree Publishing Company, [2016] |
  Series: Remarkable Lives Revealed | Includes index. |
  Audience: Ages: 7-10. | Audience: Grades: 4 to 6.
Identifiers: LCCN 2016026656 (print) | LCCN 2016027398 (ebook) |
  ISBN 9780778726890 (Reinforced library binding) |
  ISBN 9780778727002 (Paperback) |
  ISBN 9781427118103 (Electronic HTML)
Subjects: LCSH: Rudolph, Wilma, 1940-1994--Juvenile literature. |
  Runners (Sports)--United States--Biography--Juvenile literature. |
  Women runners--United States--Biography--Juvenile literature.
Classification: LCC GV1061.15.R83 M67 2016 (print) | LCC GV1061.15.
  R83 (ebook) | DDC 796.42092 [B] --dc23
LC record available at https://lccn.loc.gov/2016026656

Crabtree Publishing Company
www.crabtreebooks.com   1-800-387-7650

Printed in Canada/082016/TL20160715

**Published
in Canada**
Crabtree Publishing
616 Welland Ave.
St. Catharines, Ontario
L2M 5V6

**Published in
the United States**
Crabtree Publishing
PMB 59051
350 Fifth Ave., 59th Floor
New York, NY 10118

**Published in the
United Kingdom**
Crabtree Publishing
Maritime House
Basin Road North, Hove
BN41 1WR

**Published
in Australia**
Crabtree Publishing
3 Charles Street
Coburg North
VIC, 3058

Contents

First-Class Champion

Every person has a **unique** story. A person's story is told through a biography. Some people's biographies are famous. Other people have stories that are not as well known. We can learn a lot from any person's biography. After listening to his or her story, we may consider that person to be remarkable. Remarkable people often demonstrate certain qualities that others admire. As you read through Wilma Rudolph's biography, think about the qualities that people believe make her a remarkable person.

What is a Biography?

A biography is the story of a person's life. Biographies help us understand the experiences of others, and how their lives have been influential. They can be told through different sources of information. Primary sources include a person's own words or pictures. Secondary sources include stories from friends, family, media, and research.

Wilma Rudolph (center) proudly stood on the podium at the 1960 Summer Olympics in Rome, after winning the 100-meter race. The second-place winner was Dorothy Hyman of Great Britain, and Guiseppina Leone of Italy placed third.

Overcoming Many Obstacles

Champion runner Wilma Rudolph was the first American woman to win three gold medals at a single Olympic Games. This accomplishment didn't come without a lot of hard work, determination, and courage. As a child, Wilma wore a leg brace for **paralysis** due to illness. She was also an African American girl growing up during a time of racial **segregation** and lack of women's rights. Wilma was determined not to let these things stop her. With perseverance, she overcame these barriers and achieved her dreams.

? THINK ABOUT IT

Do you know someone that is remarkable? What qualities do they have that you admire?

History in the Making

Wilma Rudolph was born prematurely, or early, on June 23, 1940, in St. Bethlehem, Tennessee. She weighed only 4.5 pounds. Her mother and doctor feared for her life, but she survived. Her parents moved Wilma and her 21 siblings to Clarksville, where her father Ed worked as a railway **porter** and her mother Blanche cleaned the homes of wealthy white families. Wilma was a sickly child, and her mother nursed her through measles, mumps, pneumonia, and scarlet fever. Her family was poor and because they were African American, they were unable to get treatment at the local hospital where only white people were permitted.

Wilma's parents, Ed and Blanche, were very supportive of Wilma throughout her life.

A Mother's Faith

When Wilma was four years old, she became infected with **polio**, a crippling disease that left one of her legs paralyzed. Doctors said that Wilma would never walk again. Wilma's mother believed otherwise. Every week for the next two years, Wilma and her mother traveled 50 miles (80 kilometers) to the Meharry Medical College in Nashville. There, Wilma received physical therapy. She was also given a metal brace that she had to wear on her left leg and foot every day.

> "I spent most of my time trying to figure out how to get them off...But when you come from a large, wonderful family, there's always a way to achieve your goals.
>
> —**Wilma Rudolph, ESPN SportsCentury**

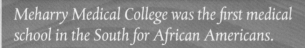

Meharry Medical College was the first medical school in the South for African Americans.

Getting Stronger Every Day

Over the next five years, Wilma's mother and older siblings massaged her leg at least four times a day. Her family believed that Wilma would one day walk without her brace. The brace made Wilma feel that she was different from other children. Her family's encouragement helped to inspire Wilma. She became determined to get stronger, and whenever she was alone, she secretly removed her brace and practiced walking without it.

This young girl has also been affected by polio. She is wearing a leg brace similar to Wilma's.

? **THINK ABOUT IT**

Wilma was determined to walk again without her brace. Using the text and quote on these pages, can you give reasons why she was so determined?

Wilma's Hard Work Pays Off

Wilma's dream to some day walk by herself came true when she was nine years old. After years of therapy and her family's encouragement, she surprised her doctors by removing the brace and walking normally. Wilma began to wear a special shoe on her left foot, and was soon playing basketball with her siblings and running races against children in her neighborhood. By the time she was twelve years old, Wilma didn't need the shoe anymore. She was able to do everything on her own!

> "
> *From that day on people were going to start separating me from that brace, start thinking about me differently, start saying that Wilma is a healthy kid, just like the rest of them.*
>
> —Wilma Rudolph, *Wilma: The Story of Wilma Rudolph*
> "

Running Like the Wind!

Wilma went to an all-black elementary school until the seventh grade. She then attended Burt High School, a new school for African-American students. She desperately wanted to play on the basketball team, but the coach did not think that she was skilled enough. She was finally allowed to play when the coach wanted her older sister on the team, and her father agreed only if Wilma was able to join as well. Wilma practiced and soon became a great basketball player. She scored so many points in her sophomore year that she set a state record.

> **"**
>
> *I ran and ran and ran every day, and I acquired this sense of determination, this sense of spirit that I would never, never give up, no matter what else happened.*
>
> **—Wilma Rudolph, *Wilma: The Story of Wilma Rudolph***
>
> **"**

The Tigerbelles

Wilma's basketball coach gave her the nickname "Skeeter" because she ran so fast on and off the court. She decided to join her school's track team, and soon caught the attention of Ed Temple, the track coach at Tennessee State University. Soon she began training with him and the students at Tennessee State. After losing every race in her first track meet, Ed invited Wilma to his summer track camp. She began running long distances every day with his racing team, called the Tigerbelles. By the end of the summer, she won all nine of her races at the National Amateur Athletic Union meet in Philadelphia.

Wilma (middle) is shown here with her coach Ed Temple and a Tigerbelles teammate.

An Olympic Feat

Wilma continued to persevere through rigorous training with the Tigerbelles team. Her training paid off when, at just sixteen years old, she qualified for the 1956 Olympics. Wilma was the youngest member of the American team. She and her teammates boarded a plane to compete at the Olympic Games in Melbourne, Australia. It was the first time Wilma had ever been on a plane, and she was excited.

Teamwork

In Melbourne, Wilma ran the third **leg**, or lap, of the 4x100-meter (m) relay race. She and her team won the bronze medal. The relay was Wilma's favorite event because of the teamwork involved. She was proud to stand on the podium with her teammates as they were awarded their bronze medals. Winning the bronze inspired Wilma to set her goals even higher—she promised herself that she would work harder to win a gold medal next.

Passing the medal

When Wilma returned from Australia, her classmates welcomed her back to school with many congratulations. They passed her medal around so that they could learn what an Olympic medal felt like.

Wilma (second from left) was awarded the bronze medal at the 1956 Olympic Games alongside her teammates (from left to right) Margaret Matthews, Mae Faggs, and Isabelle Daniels.

Gold Medal Glory

After graduating high school, Wilma enrolled at Tennessee State University in 1958. She was now an official member of the university's track team! At the Pan American Games the following year, Wilma won a silver medal in the 100m, and she and her teammates won a gold in the 4x100m relay.

*While at Tennessee State University, Wilma wanted to study elementary school education and **psychology**.*

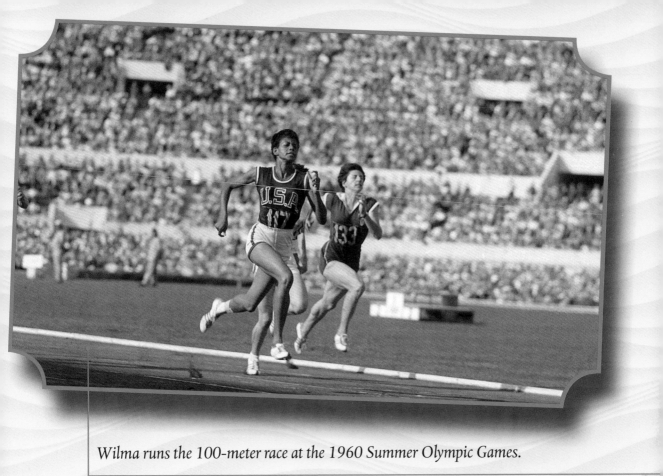

Wilma runs the 100-meter race at the 1960 Summer Olympic Games.

Reaching Her Goals

In 1960, Wilma again qualified for the Olympic Games, held in Rome, Italy. During the Games, more than 80,000 spectators filled the stadium, and the temperatures reached 100 degrees Fahrenheit (43 degrees Celsius). Despite the huge crowd and the uncomfortable heat, Wilma won the 100-meter race in just 11 seconds. She also won the 200m in 24 seconds, after running 23.2 seconds in the **semifinals**, which was a new Olympic record.

A Team Effort

After Wilma's first two gold wins, she became known as "the fastest woman in the world." But that's not all that Wilma had to show to the world. On September 11, 1960, Wilma ran the 4x100m relay with her Tennessee State teammates, Martha Hudson, Lucinda Williams, and Barbara Jones. When she ran, Wilma brought her team from behind to first place. The relay team won the race in 44.5 seconds, setting a new world record.

Wilma's inspiration in the 1960 Olympics was American track and field athlete Jesse Owens. Owens won four gold medals in the 100m, 200m, 4x100 relay, and long jump in the 1936 Olympic Games.

Three's a Charm

Winning three gold medals at the Olympic Games was not just a personal victory for Wilma, but it was also a victory for all female athletes. Wilma became the first woman in history to win that many gold medals in track and field at a single Olympic Games! People all over the world praised Wilma for her magnificent **feat**, and she quickly became the favorite athlete among the many spectators at the stadium.

Wilma holds up the three gold medals she won at the 1960 Summer Olympic Games in Rome, Italy.

Homecoming

After dominating the track events at the Olympic Games, Wilma and her teammates toured Europe with their coach Ed Temple. Wilma raced at the British Empire Games in London, England, and won every race she ran. She continued to win races throughout Europe, and massive crowds attended her races to watch her run. Wilma was now one of the most famous athletes in the world.

Wilma was an inspiration to her fans. After becoming a celebrity athlete, she often signed autographs for them.

A Hero's Welcome

When the European tour was finished, Wilma returned home to Clarksville, Tennessee, where she was welcomed with a homecoming parade that was attended by 40,000 people. During the 1960s, it was typical for public celebrations to be racially segregated, or separated. Before returning home, Wilma courageously insisted that her victory parade be open to everyone, regardless of race, or she refused to participate in it. As a result, Wilma's parade, as well as a banquet, had people of all races gathered together at one event. This was the first time in the city's history that something like this had happened.

Wilma waves to the crowd gathered at her homecoming parade in Clarksville, Tennessee.

Instant Celebrity

Wilma's perseverance inspired many people to strive for their goals, and her success made her an instant celebrity. She was invited to attend award dinners and made several television appearances. Wilma's success also earned her many awards and honors. She received the Associated Press Woman Athlete of the Year award both in 1960 and 1961, as well as the James E. Sullivan Award as the top athlete in the United States.

A Trailblazer

Wilma's achievements helped create new opportunities for female athletes in the world of sports. She was the first woman invited to compete in some of track's most prestigious events, such as the Millrose Games, where only male athletes previously competed.

Wilma was even invited by former president John F. Kennedy to a private meeting at the White House in 1961.

Back to the Grind

Even though Wilma was now a world-famous Olympic athlete, she did not become a wealthy person. At the time, it was not common for athletes to receive **endorsements**. She returned to Tennessee State University to continue her studies. She graduated in 1963. That same year, she married her high school sweetheart, Robert Eldridge, with whom she had four children, Yolanda, Djuanna, Robert Jr., and Xurry.

Wilma graduated from Tennessee State University in 1963 with a Bachelor's degree in elementary education.

Chapter 4

Back to Reality

Wilma retired from track after winning two races in a meet at Stanford University in 1962. She was just 22 years old. The next Olympic Games was just two years away, and rather than train to compete, Wilma chose not to participate. She felt that it would be best for her to end her track career on a high note, because she was unsure that she would be able to duplicate the amazing accomplishments she achieved at the Games in Rome.

Wilma ran, and won, her last race at Stanford University in California.

A New Life

Wilma found it difficult to live an everyday life after experiencing so much fame and admiration. She dedicated her time to raising her children, and had to work to take care of her family. Living back in Clarksville, she worked as a second-grade teacher at her childhood elementary school. She also coached female track athletes at Burt High School, replacing her old coach, Clinton Gray, who had tragically died in a car accident.

> "
>
> *What do you do after you are world famous and nineteen or twenty and you have sat with prime ministers, kings and queens, the Pope? Do you go back home and take a job? What do you do to keep your sanity? You come back to the real world.*
>
> **—Wilma Rudolph, *I Dream a World: Portraits of Black Women who Changed America***
>
> "

Wilma (center) was the proud mother of four children, Robert, Yolanda, Xurry, and Djuana.

Adventure Awaits!

Soon, Wilma began to travel across the United States, accepting coaching positions at different schools, and giving motivational speeches to students about working hard to reach their goals. Wilma also worked as a **broadcaster**, co-hosted a radio show, and was a sports **commentator** on television. She made sure her inspirational message was heard all over the country!

Wilma often visited schools to speak with students about following their dreams. Here, she gives a speech at the University of Pittsburgh.

Giving Back

In 1967, Wilma was invited by United States Vice President Hubert Humphrey to participate in an athletic **outreach** program called "Operation Champ." With this program, Wilma and other well-known athletes traveled to the **ghettoes** of 16 American cities to provided sports training to underprivileged children.

? THINK ABOUT IT

In what ways did Wilma use her influence as a famous athlete to make a difference in the lives of others?

During Operation Champ, Wilma taught track and field with fellow Olympian and Tennessee graduate Ralph Boston.

Wilma Rudolph Foundation

Wilma's work with Operation Champ inspired her to establish her own organization called the Wilma Rudolph Foundation. Her non-profit organization provided children with free coaching in many different sports. Wilma's foundation also offered support to children within the community with their studies at school.

> ❝
>
> *If I have anything to leave, the foundation is my legacy.*
>
> **—Wilma Rudolph**
> **The New York Times,**
> **November 13, 1994**
>
> ❞

The year before Wilma established the Wilma Rudolph Foundation, she and Robert Eldridge, her husband of 17 years, separated.

Giving all children, especially those with poor backgrounds, the chance to participate in sports was important to Wilma.

Making a Difference

In 1977, Wilma decided to publish an **autobiography** called *Wilma: The Story of Wilma Rudolph*. She believed the book would help teach others about the lessons she learned while overcoming **adversity** and illness. She also helped many organizations to open and run **inner-city** sports clubs throughout the United States, and she continued to give speeches at schools throughout the country.

On Screen

Shortly after her autobiography was published, Wilma's life story was turned into a movie. Wilma did not appear in the film, but acted as consultant while it was being shot. Actress Shirley Jo Finney played Wilma, and Denzel Washington was hired for the role of her husband Robert Eldridge. The two-hour movie aired on prime-time television on December 19, 1977, and featured actual footage of Wilma winning her three Olympic gold races.

Actress Piper Carter is shown here with Wilma Rudolph on the movie set of Wilma. *Piper played four-year-old Wilma in the movie.*

A statue of Wilma can be seen at the Tennessee Sports Hall of Fame. Her track coach Ed Temple (left) attended the grand opening of the museum in 2000.

Saying Goodbye to a Legend

On November 12, 1994, Wilma died of a brain tumor at her home in Nashville, Tennessee. She was 54 years old. Thousands of people attended her memorial service which was held at Tennessee State University, where the school's state flag was flown at half-mast in her honor. She was buried in Clarksville with the Olympic flag draped over her casket. Since her death, Wilma's life and achievements have been honored with roadways, university dormitories, and awards being named for her. Wilma's birthday, June 23, has been declared "Wilma Rudolph Day" in Tennessee.

Writing Prompts

1. What personal characteristics do you believe are important to achieve your goals? Which of these do you see in Wilma Rudolph?

2. What do you think Wilma's greatest achievement is? Why?

3. How has the story of Wilma Rudolph inspired you to strive for your own dreams?

4. Why did Wilma insist on having her homecoming celebration include people of all races? How did Wilma change people's attitudes toward racial equality?

Learning More

Books

Wilma Rudolph. Ruth Amy. Lerner Publishing Group. 2008.

Wilma Rudolph: Olympic Track Star. Lee Engfer. Capstone Press. 2006.

Wilma Rudolph: American Biographies. Stephanie Macceca. Shell Educational Publishing. 2010.

Wilma Rudolph. Isabel Martin. Capstone Press. 2014.

Wilma Rudolph: The Greatest Woman Sprinter in History. Anne Schraff. Enslow Publishing Inc. 2004.

Websites

https://espn.go.com/sportscentury/features/00016444.html
Read the story of Wilma's sports achievements on the ESPN SportsCentury website, where she was honored as one of the 50 greatest athletes of the 1900s.

www.biography.com/people/wilma-rudolph-9466552
Read Wilma's biography at Tennessee History for Kids.

www.bbc.com/sport/olympics/36508864
Watch a video of Wilma winning her three gold medals at the 1960 Olympic Games!

www.teamusa.org/News/2009/July/01/Amazing-Moments-in-Olympic-History-1960-Wilma-Rudolph
Read about Wilma Rudolph and other notable American Olympic athletes at the official website of the U.S. Olympic Hall of Fame.

Glossary

adversity Misfortune and difficulties

autobiography The story of a person's life written by that person

broadcaster Someone who presents a radio or television program

commentator Someone who presents comments on an event

diagnose To determine the identity of a disease or disorder

endorsement Giving one's public approval or support of something

feat An extraordinary act or achievement

ghetto A disadvantaged part of a city

inner-city The area of a city where mostly poor people live

leg A section of a race done in stages

outreach To provide a service to a population that would not otherwise have been accessible to them

paralysis The loss of the ability to move and/or feel a part of the body

polio A disease that affects the nerves of the spine causing the inability to move particular muscles

porter A person hired to carry luggage and other loads

psychology The science and study of the mind and behavior

segregation A policy that keeps people from different races or religions separate from each other

semifinals A round that comes before the final; the winner of which proceeds to participate in the final

unique The only one of its kind

adversity Misfortune and difficulties

Index